Fine Ham an' Haddie

Fife Council Central Area Libraries

©Fife Council Central Area Libraries
1996

ISBN 1 869984 07 2

Published by
Fife Council Central Area Libraries
East Fergus place
Kircaldy
KY1 1XT

Printed by
Cordfall Ltd
0141-332 4640

Introduction

Dialect is a very rich, expressive form of speech, which in this age of television and video is dying out, giving way to standard usage, Americanisms and Australian slang.

This booklet is an attempt to record our local use of words and phrases before they are lost and we would like to thank everyone who responded to the plea for words and meanings.

It has proved very difficult to define some of the entries. They so exactly express their meaning that, to explain the nuances of the words in other ways, was almost impossible.

We know that some words we have included are general Scottish words and phrases, so let us say this booklet charts Scots language as used in Fife. We have used the tense or part of speech in which the word is most often used.

Spelling has caused a few problems. We have standardised it where possible. Where this has proved impossible, we have used the spelling as given to us by contributors or offered alternatives.

This booklet is not a comprehensive dictionary, but a light-hearted look at Fife speech. We would be happy to hear from anyone who could add to the contents of the booklet, or could correct or add to any meanings or spellings.

James Boswell, writing in 1764, proposed to compile a dictionary of Scots because, "the Scottish language is being lost every day and in a short time will become quite unintelligible".

This is our attempt to preserve our descriptive, expressive language. We hope you enjoy it.

Contents

A'thegither, altogether

abune, above

ace hole, fireside

acht/aucht, to own; ownership e.g. let him haud the bairn that aucht the bairn; wha's acht the dug?

aff, off

affrontit, ashamed e.g. Ah'm black affrontit

afftakin', trying to ridicule; to put down

afore, before

aften, often

agin, against

agley, awry

ain, own e.g. yer ain faut

aince, once e.g. aince awa' aye awa': gone out and taking a long time to return

ainsel, myself; yourself

aipple, apple

airt, direction e.g. what airt's the wind in?: from which direction is the wind blowing?

alane, alone

ane, one

angersum, irritating

anither, another

anterin, occasional

argy bargy, argument

ashet, enamel pie dish

astreen, tonight

atween, between

auld faurent, old-fashioned

awa', away

awain, owing

aweel, okay; that's fine

Baffies, slippers

bahookey/bahookie, backside

bairge, to strut; to move clumsily; to push in

bairn, child

bandy-leggit, bow-legged

bane, bone

bannock, scone or round flat cake baked on a girdle

barkit, ingrained with dirt; encrusted

bash, blow; thump e.g. bash on the heid

bassie, wooden bowl

bauch, weak or tired; far from well

bauchle, old worn down shoe; untidy, clumsy person

bauchlie, down-at-heel

baugh, unpleasant tasting

bawbee, halfpenny

bealin', festering; furious e.g. bealin' sore; bealing temper

beedies, head lice

belter, good-looker

ben, through; in; into e.g. to go ben the room: to go into or through to another room

berfit/barefit, barefoot

besom, broom; lively, mischievous girl

bicker, to quarrel

biddy, person

bide, to remain; to live; to wait e.g. bide here: wait here; where do you bide?: where do you live?

bidie-in, someone living with another, without marriage

biggin, building

bile, to boil; boil; gastric upset

binder, strong support for the bottom of the back, made from navy blue, heavy material

birkie, lively; smart; spirited

birl, to spin

birse, temper

birsled, burnt; toasted; broiled

bits, boots

blate, bashful; modest; timid e.g. no' blate: not backward

blether, to gossip; to talk a lot of nonsense; gossip

blootered, drunk

bluid/blude, blood

bogey/boakie, dried nasal mucus

bogie, four-wheeled cart; hurlie

boke/boak/bock, to retch e.g. the dry boke: retching when there's nothing to vomit

bolster, long hard pillow

bonnie/bonny, pretty; good-looking

bookit/boukit, stature e.g. sma' bookit: small in height

borrich, messy

bow yanks, leather gaiters

brae, hill

braid, broad

brake, horse-drawn vehicle

brat, working apron

bravity, splendour; finery

braw, fine; good-looking

bree, soup

breeks, trousers

breenge, to dive in; to jump forward

brichtin, part of horse's harness

brither, brother

brizz, to force; to strain

brock, badger

broo, brow

bubbly jock, turkey-cock

bummin', bragging

bunker, work top beside the kitchen sink

bunnet/bannet, flat cap worn by men and boys

buss, clump of trees

but and ben, two-roomed house

Ca'd ower, knocked over

caddis, fluff, stoor, particularly under the bed

Cadie, flat cap

camb, comb

cannae, cannot

canny, careful

capes, grains of corn to which the chaff sticks after threshing

carfuffle, excitement; uproar

caripoutie, bandaged finger

carnaptious, cantankerous; crabbit; crochety

carriewheekit/corriefisted, left-handed

cauf, calf

cauld, cold

cauldriff, prone to feeling cold e.g. she was a cauldriff biddy: she always felt the cold

caun'le-licht, candle-light

causey, street; pavement

caw, to turn; wind e.g. caw the rope (in skipping); caw the haun'le: turn the handle

chanty, chamber pot

chap, to knock; knock

chappit, mashed; dried; cracked e.g. chappit tatties; chappit lips

check, to reprimand; to tell off

cheetie-pussie, cat

chief, friendly; intimate with someone e.g. when will I be chief with you?: when will we be friendly?

chittering, shivering with cold

chugh, tough

churls, small nuggets of coal

claes, clothes

clappit, drawn in e.g. clappit cheeks

clarty, dirty

clash, to gossip

clash-bag, gossip; tell-tale

clashmaclaver, tale telling; gossip

clausie, toilet

cleek, hook; hooked piece of iron to guide a gird as in the toy, gird and cleek; iron-headed golf club

clegs, horse-flies; gadflies

cliesh, clear

clipe, to tell tales

clippie, bus conductress

clipshear, earwig

clish-clash, idle gossip

clocher, cough; wheeze; noisy, loose cough

clockin', broody

cloor, to hit

cloot, cloth

close, vennel, open at either end, between two buildings

clout, to slap; to hit; blow; slap

cludgie, w.c.

coalie bag, carry on one's back

conferikin, everything neat and in keeping

connekit, related to; connected e.g. they were connekit through marriage

conter, contrary

contermachous, argumentative

coom, dross; coal dust

coorie, to crouch; cuddle in

corbie, crow

coup, to capsize

crabbit, bad tempered

crannie, crevice; recess

craw, to boast; crow

creel, basket; lobster trap

creenin' in, getting smaller as you grow older

cuddie, horse

cull, blockhead

cundy, drain

curnie/curnie-wurnie, pinkie

cushie/cushie doo, wood-pigeon

cutty-sark, short under-shirt

Dad, beat; hit e.g. I'll gie ye a dad in the lug: I'll hit you on the ear

daud, lump; quantity

daunder/daunner, to stroll; stroll

daur, dare e.g. daurna: dare not

dee, die

de'il, devil

dementit, very worried

denner, dinner

dey, grandad

dicht, wipe e.g. dicht yer neb: wipe your nose

diddle, to cheat; to bounce a baby up and down on your knee

dirl, to stun; to hit; smack e.g. dirl on the lug: smack on the ear

dishle, street gutter

divit, sod; piece of turf

dochle, fool

dochter, daughter e.g. guid-dochter: daughter-in-law

dock, bottom, backside

docken, type of weed e.g. docken leaf

doidle, to bounce a baby up and down on your knee

doitered/doited/doutit, senile; muddled; half-mad

donnert, stupid

doo, pigeon

dook, to swim; to duck; swim e.g. dookin' for aipples: ducking for apples at Halloween

dookin', soaking

dorty/in the dorts, in the huff; sulking

douk, to duck; to avoid

doup/doupie/dowt, cigarette end

dour, sullen

dover, to doze off

dowry clout, skinned knee or other minor injury which required adult sympathy and a bandage

drammlick, small piece of oatmeal dough stuck to the bowl

dreich, dull; miserable

drookit, drenched

dross, small change; small coal

drouthy, thirsty

dub, puddle

duddie, dog with matted hair

duggit, matted; thickened by shrinking e.g. duggit jumper

dunderheid, stupid person

dunt, knock

Easy osy, not bothered either way; easy going

eeksie-peeksie, equal shares; all things being equal

een, eyes

Fairy tickles/fernitickles, freckles

fankle, muddle

fantoosh/fantoush, flashy; fancy; ultra-fashionable

fash, to fret; to worry; to bother

fashious/fascious, troublesome; not easily pleased

fauld, to fold

faut, to fault; fault

feardie gowk, frightened person

feart, frightened

fecht, to fight; fight

feechit, disgusting

feichalin', fidgeting

feloorie, fit; fright

feltyfleer, fieldfare

fikey, finnicky

fit, foot

fitba', football

flech, flea

flechy, covered with fleas

fleg, fright

flit, to move house

flooers/flo'ers, flowers

flype, loose piece of skin

flyte, to scold

foggiebummer, bumble bee

foosty/foostit, stale; mouldy

footlin', small

forbye, besides

forfochen/firfochen/fair forfochen, tired out

fornent, in front of

forrit, forward

fow-tow, full up; replete

fower, four

frae, from

freend, friend

frythe, to fry; frying pan

fu', full

fum, clumsy person

fushionless, gormless

fyle, to soil; to defile

Gallus/gallous, brass necked

galluses, braces

galoot, idiot

gant, to yawn; yawn

ganzie, jersey

gar, to make e.g. gar ye grue: make you sick

gaun, going e.g. ah'm gaun oot

gaup/gawp, to stare open-mouthed

gawk, to stare

gee gaw, cheap trinket

gibbles, bits and pieces

gi'e, to give e.g. gi'e's a shot: give me a turn

gimp/jimp, tight; close-fitting

girl, to shudder with fear; have your teeth set on edge

girn, to cry; moan e.g. girny bairn

gitter, to mess about; messy worker

gittergaw, hack between the toes

gittering, wasting time

gitters, mud

glaid-e'ed, squint eyed

glaikit, daft

glaur, mud

glower, to frown; to scowl; to stare intently

glumsh, sulky, sullen mood; lover's quarrel

gomerel/gommeril, idiot; fool

goonie, nightgown

govie dick, goodness gracious

gowan, daisy; wild marguerite

gowff, golf

gowk, fool e.g. hunty gowk: when you catch someone out with an April Fools joke you shout "hunty gowk"

Gowksday, April 1st

graip, garden fork

graith, lather; miner's tool e.g. soapy graith: soapy water; gi'e a graith: wash clothes before putting them in the boiler

grauvit, scarf

grippit, holding yourself in because you're bursting to go to the toilet

grozers, gooseberries

gruppie, tight-fisted

guddle, to dabble with the fingers, especially in dirt or water; muddle; mess

guid-sister, sister-in-law

gully, large knife

gumption, fighting spirit; common sense; get up and go

gundie, old bicycle

gutties, gym shoes

gutty/guttie, catapult

gyte, daft; not all there e.g. gaun gyte: going out of your mind

Hack, cut on the finger which won't heal

hackit, ugly

haddies, haddocks

ha'e, have

hafflin', youthful; half-grown

haik, to scrounge; horse; cart

haimes/hames, part of a horse's harness

hairst, harvest

hale/hail, whole

half chist, half way down

hallan, inner wall; door

hame-wan, homesick; homeward bound

hap, to cover up; to keep warm; warm outer clothing

happit, wrapped up

harpin' on about, nagging

hashie, careless; slovenly; hard on clothing

haud, hold e.g. haud yer horses: wait a minute

hauf, half

hauf loaf, loaf baked in a double loaf tin e.g. twa hauf loafs: two loaves baked together

haund, hand

haun'le, handle

haver, to talk nonsense

havers, nonsense; rubbish

heid yin, boss

heelie, proud; arrogant

hen, dear; darling; pet

hen taed, having turned in toes

hilter-skilter, helter-skelter; heedless

hingy, off colour before becoming ill; under the weather

hippin, nappy

hippit, stiff from being in one position too long

hirple, to hobble

hives, weals; skin eruptions

hoast, cough

hoody craw, hooded crow

hoose end, fat; broad e.g. she's like a hoose end

horneygolach/horneygoloch, earwig

hoolets/howlets, owls

howk, to dig

howkit, dug up

humphy-backit, hunchbacked

hunkers, thighs

hurcheon/hurchin, hedgehog

hurdies, haunches; hips e.g. he hadnae the hurdies for a kilt

hurl, wee run in a car or on a bike; push e.g. hurl a pram

hurlie, bogie; four wheeled cart

Icket, ear of corn

ilka, each; every

ill-aff, poor

ill-gainshoned/ill-gaishoned, mischievous

ill shapit, misshapen

ingin, onion

ingle, fireplace; fire burning on a hearth

intil, inside

isnae, is not

Jag, prick with a sharp instrument; injection

jalouse, to guess; to suppose

jeckdaa, jackdaw

jeely piece, jam sandwich

jessie pont, effeminate man

jiggered, exhausted; broken

jiggery pokery, suspicious goings-on

jings/by jings, expression of surprise

jink, to dodge

jist, to jest; just

jook/jouk/jouck, to duck; side step

Kail, soup; broth e.g. pat o' kail: pot of soup

kain/ken, to know e.g. ah dae ken: I don't know

keek, to peep

keeker, black eye

kilt, to overturn

kindlin', sticks; wood to start a fire

kirn, churn

kist, trunk

kitchen, savoury tea-time meal

kitlin, kitten

kittle, to puzzle; to perplex

kittly, itchy

knab, snob; important person

kye, cattle

kyte, stomach

Lad/ lawd, boyfriend

laggered wi', thickly spread with

laich, low

lane, lone

lang, long

lang-luggit, wily; shrewd; eavesdropper

leave piece, playtime snack

leerie, light; lamp-lighter; cunning

limmer, rascal; wayward child

lip, impudence

lippen, to depend; to trust; to take a liking to

lippie/leepy o' tatties, 7lbs of potatoes

lobby, hall

loup, to jump

loupin/lowpin, someone crawling with lice or fleas

lousy-arnot, earth nut

low/lowe, flame; light

lowse, to free; to loosen

lowsin' time, finishing time at work

lug, ear

luggy, three legged stool for milking

lum, chimney

lum heid, highest point of the roof

lunt, to walk with a spring; to walk briskly

Maggotty, difficult to please

maik/maick, halfpenny

mak' a sham, to pretend

manky, dirty

mant, to stammer

married ontae, married to

mask, to infuse tea

mauchy/maucht/maukit, clammy; foul; dirty

maullicater, tough, mean person

maun, must

mealie moothed, smarmy

messages, shopping

messan, small dog (used contemptuously)

mim-moothed, prim; demure way of speaking or eating

min, moon

mingin', smelling badly; drunk

mingy, mean; greedy; miserly

mirk, dark; obscure; black

misca', to miscall; to abuse verbally

mittens, gloves with only a thumb

moanin' minnie, complainer

mony/monny, many; lots

mooch, to scrounge; to beg

mou', mouth

mouldieworts/mowdieworts, moles; molehills

muck, dung e.g. muck midden: dung heap

muckin'/muck'n, filthy; dirty

muckle, large quantity; big

muffies, moths

mumpin', complaining

mun, must

mutch, woman's linen or muslin cap

Nabbit, caught suddenly or unexpectedly

napper, head

neb, nose

neeps, turnips

nettie, woman wool collector

neuk, corner

nice gabbit, fussy about food

nicher, to neigh; laugh contemptuously

nicket, caught; cut off

niffer, to exchange; to barter

nive/nieve/neeve/neive, fist; handful

no' bad, fairly well; all right

nocht, nothing

nock, clock e.g. toon nock: town clock

noo, now

nowt/nout, oaf; bumpkin

nunks, apples

nunking, stealing apples

Ongaun, uproar

oorie, damp, shivery weather

ooze, fluff

ower-bye, over there

oxter, armpit

Pain in the peenie, tummy pain

pairt, small piece of land

palaver, fuss

parritch, porridge

partan, crab

pauchle, to fiddle money

paund/paunds, vallance around a bed to hide what's underneath; curtains hung from the base of the bed to the floor

pawkies, mittens; gloves with only a thumb

pawky, sooky

pech/pecht, to pant

peebed/pee the bed, dandelion

peekit, sickly; pale

peenge, to whine; to complain

peenie/peeny, apron

peerie, spinning-top

peerie-heels, high heels

peeweep, lapwing

perjink, just so!

pernickity/pernickety, particular; fussy

peckle, little

pickle, muddle; small quantity

piler, boy's homemade cart

pingle/pinglie, finicky

pingled, overcome with exhaustion

pirn o' threed, reel of thread

placket fastener, stud

plackless, penniless

plaisterin', in a slapdash way

platch, piece of cloth

plook, pimple

plot, to put an infected finger in boiled water to draw the poison

plowt, to soak; potted meat; hough

pluchie/pleuchie, ploughman

podley, small coal fish

poke, paper bag

poulie, louse; flea

pouthered, powdered

pow, head

preen, pin

press, cupboard

puckle, small amount

puddock, frog

puggie, monkey

puggled, exhausted

puir, poor

pulley, clothes airer made from wooden slats, suspended from the ceiling

purley pig, piggy bank

Rakin', searching untidily

ranty, merry

rascal fair, hiring market for male workers who had failed to find employment at the regular market

rax, to strain

redd, to tidy up; to clean up

reek, to smoke; smoke

reenge, to search

richt, right

rigbody, part of a cart horse's harness

riggin, rafters

rile, to upset; to anger

rime, hoar frost; frosty haze

rizzard, clothes half-dried from the sun - fine for ironing

rookit, broke; cleaned out; no money

roset, resin

roup, auction

row, to wind

rummle-gumption, common-sense; level-headedness

runkled, wrinkled

runt, core of an apple

Saft, soft

sair, sore

saithe, full-grown coalfish

saps, invalid food of bread and sugar soaked in hot milk

sark/serk, shirt e.g. workin' serk: work shirt

saut, salt

saumon, salmon

scaffy, dustman

scart, to scratch

scaul/scawl, to scold; scold

schule, school

scodge, servant; drudge

scooched, slipped

scud, blow; slap; naked

scuff, to graze e.g. scuff your shoes: take the top layer of leather off

scullery, kitchen

scunner/skunner, to disgust; nuisance

scunnered, fed up

scunnersome, sickening

seamaw/seamew, seagull

semmit/simmit, vest

shauchly, down at heel; untidy

shavie, trick

shears/sheers, scissors

shed, hair parting

sheel, shovel

sheugh, ditch

shilpit, pinched looking; weak; scrawny

shin/shune/shoon, shoes

shoo, to sew

shoogle, to shake

shuch/sheuch, hips e.g. short i' the shuch: short in stature

siccar, sure e.g. mak siccar: make sure

siver, road drain

skale, to spill

skedaddle, to push off

skeerie, restive

skeilly, slate pencil

skelb/skelf, splinter

skelly-e'ed, cross-eyed; having a squint

skelp, to slap; to smack

skelping, spanking

skilt, spilled

skite, to slip; blow e.g. skite aff the lug: slap on the ear

skoosh, to squirt; lemonade

skoot, to squirt

skraich, high-pitched scream

slaister, to make a mess; messy person

slaisters, dirty slops

slaver, to drool; to talk nonsense

sleekit, sly

slerp, to eat noisily e.g. dinna slerp yer soup

slider, ice cream wafer

slouter/slouster, to work in a slovenly way

smeddum, spirit; mettle; liveliness

smit, to catch the same ailment; to have the same problem e.g. to get the smit: to be infected with

smousterin', eating greedily, especially sweets

snab, cobbler

sneck, door-latch

snell, cold; piercing; biting e.g. snell wind

snib, catch; small bolt to fasten a door

snochering, snoring; snorting

socht, looked for

sonsie, plump; jolly

sook, to suck

soople, supple

sooricks, docken leaves

souff, to blow gently; sigh e.g. the wind souffs up the pend

soup/soop, to sweep

sowel, soul e.g. puir sowel: poor soul

spaiver, opening in the front of trousers

speir, to ask e.g. she was speirin' for ye

speug/spug, house-sparrow

spune, spoon

spurtle, porridge stick

stave, sprain

stays, corset

stech, steep

stechy/steuchie, stiff-jointed

steck/steek, to sew; to close; stick e.g. steek the door: shut the door

steer, to stir

steerie, restless; lively; causing commotion e.g. steerie bairn

stell, still for whisky

stervin', starving; hungry

stoatin', very drunk

stookie, plaster cast on a broken limb

stoondin', throbbing

stoor/stour, dust

stot, to bounce e.g. stot the ba'

stramash, fuss; uproar

stravaging, strolling; wandering aimlessly

stretcher, wooden pole for pushing the clothes line higher up

stuckie, starling

sweirt, reluctant; loath

synd, to rinse

syne, since; then; ago

Tackets, hobnails e.g. tackety boots, hobnail boots

taes, toes

taigle, to hinder; entangle

tammie-norrie, puffin

tapsalteerie, topsyturvy

tarry-fingered, light fingered

tattie pickin'/ tattie howkin', potato harvesting

tattiebogle, scarecrow; stupid

tawse, leather belt for punishment at school

teabread, cookies; buns

teuchter, Highlander; country lad

theel, porridge stick

thole, to tolerate; to bear

thrapple, throat

thrawn, stubborn; twisted

threep/thrip, to argue; insist on; strong opinion

tike/tyke, hair mattress; naughty, dirty wee boy

tim, to empty; to pour out e.g. to tim out the teapot: to empty the teapot

tober, to beat; to thrash; to quarrel

tod, fox

toorie/tourie, woollen bonnet; top-knot of hair

tooried, muddled e.g. ah'm a' tooried up: I'm all mixed up

tousie/toozie, tousled

trauchled/trachled, burdened; over-worked; fatigued

tulzie, quarrel

tum'le, to fall

tumshy/tumshie, turnip

twel'month, year

Unce, ounce

unco, very; extremely

Wa', wall

wabbit/wabbit oot, tired out e.g. ah'm fair wabbit: I'm tired out

wadna, would not

wairsh/wirse, tasteless; insipid

wallop, to beat; to thrash; blow

wame, stomach

wappie, wasp

wast, west e.g. wast the kirk: west of the church

wauch/waugh, musty; stale

waukerife/waukrife, wakeful e.g. waukerife bairn: wakeful child

waur, worse e.g. the waur o' the wear: the worse for wear

wearyin', longing; yearning e.g. I'm wearyin' to see her: I'm longing to see her

wecht, weight

wee, small amount; small

weskit, waistcoat

whang, thong, large piece or slice e.g. whang o' cheese; large piece of cheese

whaup, curlew

whaur, where

wheelin', coarse, worsted yarn

wheen, several; quite a few

wheesht/whist, be quiet e.g. hud yer wheesht: stop talking

whiles, sometimes; now and then

whitterock/whittrick/whutterick, curlew; weasel; furtive, small weasel-faced person

wiselike/wicelike, good; decent

wimplin', winding; meandering of a river

winching/wenching, dating; courting e.g. are you winching?: are you going steady?

winna/winnae, will not

worset/wurset, worsted yarn

wrocht, worked e.g. he wrocht at the mill; hard wrocht

Yaird, yard in length; garden

yellow-yite/yellow-yoit/yella yite, yellow-hammer

yestreen, last night

yet/yett, gate; natural pass between hills e.g. Yetts o' Muckhart

yince/yinst, once

yow/yowe, ewe

PHRASES

A'body kens what to dae wi' a drucken wife, but him that's got ain, theory and practice are very different

A' Jock Tamson's bairns, all equal

A' tae wallops, everything wrong, especially with one's health; powerful beats of the heart

A'thing ta'en awa', hysterectomy

A' you in there for here come oot an if you're no' in there for here, bide in, cry of guard at Dysart station during the war when there were no signs at stations and he had forgotten which station the train had arrived at.

Ah'm that hungry, ah cud eat a store horse atween twa bread vans, expression of extreme hunger

Aince errant, to come specially to deliver a message or parcel e.g. did you come aince errant or were you coming anyway?

Anour/anower the bed, in the bed e.g. it's easier tae get anower an' atower the bed when just the heid o' the bed's agin the wa': it's easier to get in and out of bed when the head of the bed is against the wall.

As licht as pipe reek, not the full shilling

At the lyin' in, at the baby's birth

Atour/atower the bed, out of the bed.

Auld claes and parritch, back to the routine; back to work after a holiday

Auld maid's bairns are aye the best brocht up, referring to someone who thinks they are an authority on something they know nothing about

Awa' an' chase yerself, no chance; get lost

Awa' wi' ye, suggests that although you do not believe what is said, there may be some truth in it; sceptical response

Awfie ill pit thegither, not tidy; thrown together; mess

Aye gaun yersel' then?, how are you?

Bonnie face sets a dish cloot, if you're good looking you can wear anything

Ca' me what ye like but dinna ca' me ower, call me whatever you like but don't knock me over (play on the word ca')

Cauld kail het up, second day vegetable soup

Causey saint and a hoose de'il, well behaved outside, the opposite at home

Clocher'n an' hoastin', coughing and spluttering

Cobbler's bairns are aye the worst shod, someone who is so busy working for others they have no time or inclination to see to themselves or to their family

Come awa' ben, come in; welcome

Comin' doon hale water, pouring rain

Connekit through drink, drinking partner

Coo quacks of May, short spell of bad weather in May, when the cattle bellow with the cold easterly haar

Coo's tail, always last e.g he's aye at the coo's tail

Couthie and cosy, warm and comfortable

Cowardy custard, taunt of cowardice; afraid

Creaking gate hings langest, the one who is always ailing lives longest

Croon the cuddy, the last straw e.g. that croon'd the cuddy: that was the last straw

Deid lice fa'n aff her, slow and couldn't care less; bone idle

De'il a fear, to hell with it; no fear; not a bit of it

Did ye get a click?, did you meet someone? e.g. at the dancing, did you get walked home? colloquially "fixed up"

Dinna dreep on your gebbie, while eating, don't drop or spill your food

Dinna fash yersel', don't fret yourself; don't worry

Dinna speir the road ye ken, if you already know, why ask?; don't ask when you know already

Div ah no?, do I not?

Doo daft, pigeon fancier

Doo's cleckin, two children, a son and a daughter

Dorty pooches, sulky broo, when will I be chief with you?, chanted to someone who is sulking asking when they will be friendly again

Dour mutt, sulky person

Drappin' drouth, fine drizzle

Dree yer ain weird, go your own way; live your own life; suffer the consequences of your actions

Drookit rat, drenched; like a drowned rat

Drouth/drouthy, thirst; thirsty

Dry nod wis a' he said, the usual greeting was 'Aye' - to omit it and only nod was showing displeasure

Easy-caulded, subject to head colds

Easy kittled, easy coorted, easy made a fule o', man daft

Eat up yer at yer auntie's and she's blund, help yourself; feel free

Erse fur elby, back to front

Face like a p'isoned pup, sour-faced

Face like a puttin' stot, sour-faced

Face like a torn sark, grumpy expression

Face like a torn scone, dorty or sulky face

Fine drouth, good drying weather

Fine ham an' haddie, pretty pickle

Folk ken their ain kin best, people know their own business best

Fu' as a puggie, the worse for drink; drunk

Gang yer ain gait, go your own way

Gantin's wantin', yawning because you are hungry

Gar ye grue, make you sick

Gaun aboot folk/gaun aboot buidy, idle people/idle person, always going about but not working

Gaun fit's aye gittin', if you are always on the look out you will always find something

Gey faur through, near death

Gey peelie wally, pale and ill-looking

Gi'e it laldy, get stuck in

Gi'en me gip, paining me a lot

Greetin' teeny, whinger

Guid gear comes in sma' bu'k, because something is small doesn't mean it's not good or worthwhile: good things come in small amounts

Guid goad a' michty, exclamation of irritation or surprise

Gut's like a wa' press, huge appetite

Had a dizzie, been stood up

Hantle sicht worse, lot worse

Hard up, soor dook, ye canna throw a happeny oot, taunt of meanness - usually from a child

He maun hing as he grows, colloquially - he can stick!

He wid skin a loose for its tally, he would skin a louse for its tallow i.e. greedy and mean

He widnae gi'e ye a thick penny for a thin ane, he's very mean

Head like a divit, tousled head

Heid bummer, manager; prominent or important person

Hen on a het girdle, nervous and jumpy

Hens march to the midden, everyone moving at once, irregularly

Her ain name/tae her ain name, her maiden name

Here ye are for whar yer gaun. A you yins in there for here come oot, heard at Buckhaven railway station

He's a' the man he'll ever be, he'll never change; never get any better

He's been here afore, he's had a previous life, describing a precocious child

He's failed wi' a fu' pooch, despite all his advantages, he's failed

His eggs are a' double yocket, he's always boasting ; his things are better than any one else's; he's making out that things are better than they really are

His pooches are a' shewed up, he's slow to take his turn to pay

How's a' the sair bits? Daein' awa' or going awa'?, how are you today? Often heard in Links Library!

Hud yer wheesht, be quiet!

Hunger's guid kitchen, if you are hungry anything tastes good

I cannae sowther wi' her, I can't get on with her; I can't be doing with her

If he fell in the harbour he'd come oot wi' his pooches fu' o' fish, he's always lucky; things always work out well for him

If ye dinna speir ye'll no' ken, if you don't ask you won't know

If ye werena' yucky, ye widna' claw, if you weren't so dirty, you wouldn't scratch; if the cap fits, wear it

If ye yase what ye ha'e ye'll never want, make use of what you have

If you're no gaw gan, then ah'm no gaw gan, if you are not going to go, then I am not going to go

In bed like spunes in a drawer, tucked in like spoons lying on their sides

Ingin Johnnie, onion seller

It jist taks a niffie o' stoor tae mak' a gowpen o' glaur, small piece of gossip is, by repitition, blown up into a great scandal

It'll see me oot, it will last my lifetime, said by the elderly seeing no reason to replace an article

It's a puir body that's no' missed, it's a lonely person who will not be missed by someone

It's a sair fecht wi' ither folks' bairns, other folk's children are worse than your own, often said sarcastically

It's jist a sham, pretence

It's no' what ye ha'e, it's what ye dae wi' what ye ha'e, you don't have to have much as long as you use it well and make the most of it

It's yer meat that mak's ye bonny, you have a well-rounded figure - a sign of being comfortably off

Just a slaver thro' the wind, drizzle

Just gi'e's a cry in the passin', just drop in when you are passing; don't wait for an invitation;

Knotless threid, aimless

Lady Muck frae Stoorie Castle, someone who puts on false airs and graces

Lang drink o' watter lookin' for a tumbler, aimless; lost; gormless

Lang may yer lum reek, may everything keep going well for you; hope everything goes well with you

Like a haddie waitin' for a tattie, lost and gormless looking

Long luggit bairn, child who's always listening in to adult conversations

Ma jumper's a' scaumed, my jumper is matted and washed in

Mair ye eat, the bigger the dividend, Co-op Society dividend was calculated on amount spent, so the more groceries you ate the bigger the dividend

Many a mickle mak's a muckle, lots of little things mount up to a lot

May yer girnal aye be lippin', may your cupboard always be full to the brim

Maybe aye and maybe hooch aye, expression of disbelief, or scepticism

Mooth like a drawn purse, pursed up lips; sour-faced

Nae sicca thing, no such thing

Ne'er cast a cloot till May's oot, don't take winter clothes off until after May blossom comes out

No' worth a docken, worthless

Oxterin' and huddin' haunds, courting

Palin' stabs, fence posts

Pan loaf, most people bought batch baked "plain loaf". A miner's piecebox was a long narrow shape to take the slices. Tin or pan baked bread was regarded as "better class" and this became linked with "talking proper" and so was known as talking "pan loaf" — a source of amusement as mistakes were frequent.

Paralysis of the galluses and heart disease in the stays, reply when asked what was wrong with someone who was a hypochondriac i.e. paralysis of the braces and heart disease in the corsets

Park yer knitting, take a seat

Pit the wuid in the hole, shut the door

Putty an' pent huds mony a rent, papering over the cracks doesn't really solve the problem

Row up the nock, wind up the clock

Sair fecht, struggle

Sair haund, large piece of bread and jam held in one hand

Sair heidie, type of cake with a paper band round it

Save yer ain fish guts for yer ain sea mews, make provision for your own

Scairdey gowk, someone who is cowardly or frightened

Scoor oot/poor out/scramble, money thrown by the bride's father from the wedding car, for local children

Scuffin' clothes, working clothes; ordinary clothes

See how the bools rowe, see how the bowls run; wait and see what will happen

Shakin's o' the poke, last born child

She blethers like a book withoot batters, she never stops talking; she goes on like a book without covers

She looks like a washed oot dish cloot, she looks pale and tired

She pits her beads on tae dad her rugs, she gives herself airs and graces

She'd fa' oot wi' the stanes in the wa', she'd fall out with anybody over anything, for no reason

Sheepie mehs, common white clover; child's name for a sheep

She's no' tae be lippen tae, she's not to be talked back to

Shiff o' braid, slice of bread

Shoot the craw, go away; leave

Shufflin' gitters, snoring

Skelp yer doup, smack your bottom

Skiddlin' guddlin', playing with water

Skinnin' cauld, cold enough to take the skin off you

Skite ower, to dust quickly

Sky's hingin' laich in the crap wa', it's going to rain, the clouds are low

Sma' coal, dross to damp the fire

Smeekit oot, smoked out; full of smoke

Snottery beek, dirty nose

Snottie nosed, stuck up

Soor dook, sour milk; sour, mean person; crying face.

Sow's wallops, marshmallows

Steevie beef, squares of jellied oil for lino

Stey brae, steep hill

Sticky willies, sticky creepers from willow trees

Stoot hert tae a stey brae, stout heart to a steep brae; strong heart overcomes difficulties

Swagger that wid dry a washin', cocky, strutting walk

Tae gar fils speir an' you're the first ane, to make fools ask and you are the first one (retort to a persistent questioner)

Tak' a line, take a shopping list

Tak' an' speak richt, speak correctly; do not use dialect

Teeny fae the neeps/Teeny fae Troon/Teen Parish, untidy, dishevelled person

There's a bit o' blue big enough to mend a pair o' breeks, break in the rain clouds enough to lead to better weather

There's aye a slippy stane at ilka body's door, everybody has their problems; pride goes before a fall

There's very little in the pow that lichts the caun'le at the low/them that lichts a caun'le at a low has nae muckle in their pow, comment on a stupid action

They think theirsel' nae sma' drink, they have a good conceit of themselves

Things maun aye be some wey, fatalistic acceptance of things as they are

Through the room/ben the hoose, in the next room

Ticht fistit, mean; greedy with money

Tig-toyin', e.g. Tam's tig-toyin' with Maggie: Tam's having an affair with Maggie

Tongue that wid clip cloots, virago; sharp tongued

Tripe and trollywaggers, unshapely, corpulent person

Twa nebs in the poke, twa horses in the yoke, if duties are shared then the priviliges must be shared

Twa ply reek/twa ply o' reek, very slim

Up afore yer claes wis on, bit ahead of yourself

Want aboot him, not the full shilling

Wantin' a nut, having a screw loose

Weel kent/weel kenned, well known e.g. she has a weel kent face: she is well known

We're no' awa' tae bide awa', we will be back

What's for ye'll no' gan' by ye', what will be will be; life's path is marked out

What's guid tae gi'e shidnae be ill tae tak, do unto others; if you dish it out you should be able to take it

When are ye better?, when is the baby due?

When did ye fa'?, when did you become pregnant?

Whither or no', out of sorts

Wipe the gitters aff yer kilt and come and ha'e a dram, clean yourself up and come out for a drink

Wire in, to tuck in to food; to get on with work

Wyle weel, to pass the time well

Ye canna' see green cheese but yer een birl/reel, you want everything; envious of everything

Ye canna' tak the breeks aff a Heilandman, you can't have what doesn't exist

Ye great muckle sumph, you great lump

Ye never even said "collie will ye lick", you never even offered me a bit

Ye see it a', the answer to "how are you?", it means so-so

Ye'll get sent awa' wi' the wee yella van, you'll be sent to the madhouse

Yer a sicht for sair een, I'm pleased to see you

Yer een's bigger than yer belly, you have taken a larger portion of food than you are able to eat

Yer een's connekit tae yer bladder, you cry easily

Yer fishin' but yer line's no' long enough, you're prying but you'll not find out

Yer heid gi'es yer feet a lot o' work/little in the heid's hard on the feet/little wit intae the heid mak's muckle trauchle tae the feet, if you don't think things through you give yourself twice the work

Yer like a coo wi' a gun, extremely clumsy

Yer like naebody's bairn, untidy; unkempt

Yer tongue taigles yer feet, you talk too much and it stops you working

Yer writin's like a hen scartin' in the midden, your writing is illegible

Ye've made a richt Wullie's bannet o' that, you've made a right mess of that

Yokin' time, starting time at work; start an activity

MINING

Airms like a brusher

Beet knee, miner's version of housemaid's knee

Coal heughs, pit shafts - shallow holes of about 25ft

Cods, bearing of a hutch axle

Glennie, safety lamp for testing for the presence of gas

Ingawn e'e, entrance to a drift mine or coal seam at the surface outcrop, where the seam is not entered vertically

Moleskins, strong, durable trousers worn underground

Monkey brae

Up sugh and doon shally

PLACES

Anster, Anstruther

Auld bucket pats, salt pans near Kirkcaldy harbour

Awa' tae Freuchie, away you go. From the days when someone was banished from the royal court at Falkland and sent to Freuchie

Buckhyne, Buckhaven

Carryin' saut to Dysart and puddings to Tranent, Scottish version of carrying coals to Newcastle i.e. carrying out a redundant task

Dysart for coal an' saut, Pathhead for meal an' maut, Kirkcaldy for lassies braw, Kinghorn for breakin' the law

Freuchie where the craws fly backwards tae keep the stoor oot o' their een

The Galt'n, Gallatown

He needs a lang-shanket spoon that sups kail wi' the De'il or a Fifer, few people thought to be as cunning and wily as Fifers are - be on one's guard with such people

He that will to Cupar, maun to Cupar, if someone is determined on a course of action there is no stopping him

I'll gar yer lugs ding like a Culross griddle, I'll make your ears ring like the sound of iron being made into a griddle

I'll see you in Cupar on Tuesday, that being market day and a meeting place

Kirkcaldy heist, getting the heave; being thrown out (derives from linoleum factories' high waste chute)

The Methil, unique Fife way of referring to Methil

She has mair faces than the Gallatown clock, she is two-faced

Some say that the Deil's deid and buried in Kirkcaldy, some say he'll rise again and dance the Heiland Laddie

The Wemyss, unique Fife way of referring to Wemyss

GAMES AND ACTIVITIES

Bools, marbles

British Bulldog, hop on one leg, with arms folded, try to bump into someone else and make them put both feet on the ground

Buddie, pick rosebuds from someone's garden, throw them at their door and run

Cat and dog, a piece of wood tapered at both ends was laid in the gutter, resting on the pavement. You hit it with a stick and when it flew up, you tried to keep it in the air by hitting it with the stick

Chap door run, ring someone's door bell and then run away

Cocky Dunty, game where each boy carried another on his back and each pair tried to unseat their opponents

Dreep the dyke, hanging full stretch from the top of a wall then letting yourself go

Doublers, throwing two balls against the wall in turn

Haud ye up ma cuddy/haunch cuddy haunch/cuddies wechts, two teams are formed. The smallest person in one team is chosen as the "pillow", holding on to a wall or railings. The rest of the team line up behind him, bending down, holding on to each other at the waist. The second team take it in turn to jump on to the backs of the first team, trying to break the "cuddies" back

Headers, keeping the ball in the air by heading it; boys would head the ball against the Raith Rover's football club sign until they missed, when they made way for the next boy. When played on the sands, if you scored a goal you got two points, if the goal keeper headed it he got one point

Hide and Seek, a call of "Fife free block" would free those caught

Hoist the white flag, a boy/girl was given a five minute head start. He/she ran off, marking arrows on the road for the others to follow. He/she then had to evade the others, double back and get to the start without being caught

Keepie-up, keeping a ball in the air with knees, head or feet

Kerbie, hitting a ball against the kerb

Kick the can, version of hide and seek where a can is kicked and the time taken by the person who is to seek, in picking it up, determines the time the others have to hide

Leeve oh!, chasing and capturing people to put in a den, then someone runs in, shouts "Leeve oh!", and frees them

McCreadie says, a version of "Simon says"

Mair gress, term used in lawn bowls, telling the bowler to take a wider line

Paldies/Peevers, version of hopscotch

Raggyin', dribbling the ball as in football

MISCELLANY

Get up auld wife and dinna be sweir, Gi'e me a cake as long as yer here/The day will come when I'll be deid/You'll never want for cake nor breid

Ma feet's cauld ma shin's thin/Gi'e's ma cake and let me rin, New Year's rhyme from Anstruther/Cellardyke

Tell Ben tae come ben. If Ben disnae come ben, tell Ben that I'll be ben to bring Ben ben, tongue twister

Oh dear me
Ma granny caught a flea
She sauted it an' peppered it
An' had it fir her tea
Ma granny didnae like it
So she gi'ed it tae me
Ah didnae like it
So Ah flung it in the sea

When Falkland Hill puts on his cap, the Howe of Fife will get a drap and when the Bishop draws his cowl, look out for wind and weather foul

A Polish soldier billeted in a Scottish home during the war, asked how he was coping with the language, said "All right", but two words had him puzzled. 'Yup' and 'Mup'. "In what context were they used?" asked the friend. "Well", says he, "My landlady stands at the foot of the stairs every morning and shouts 'Yup' and the daughter upstairs yells down 'Mup', in other words "Are you up" and "Yes, I'm up"

The story is told of two Scots who met while abroad. "Where are you from?", said the first.

"I'm from Scotland", said the other.

"Gi'e's yer haund", said the first, "So am I. Where do you come from?"

"From Fife", said the other.

"In that case, gi'e's baith yer haunds", said the first, referring to the reputation Fifers have for being fly, the first man wanted to see both his hands to see what he was up to

"I'll tell ye a story aboot wee Jockie Norrie if ye'll no speak in the middle o' it. Will ye no'?"

A child invariably answers, "No", to be told, "That's it, you spoke".

I'll tell ye a story
Aboot wee Jockie Norrie
Who lived up a closie
And in a wee doorie